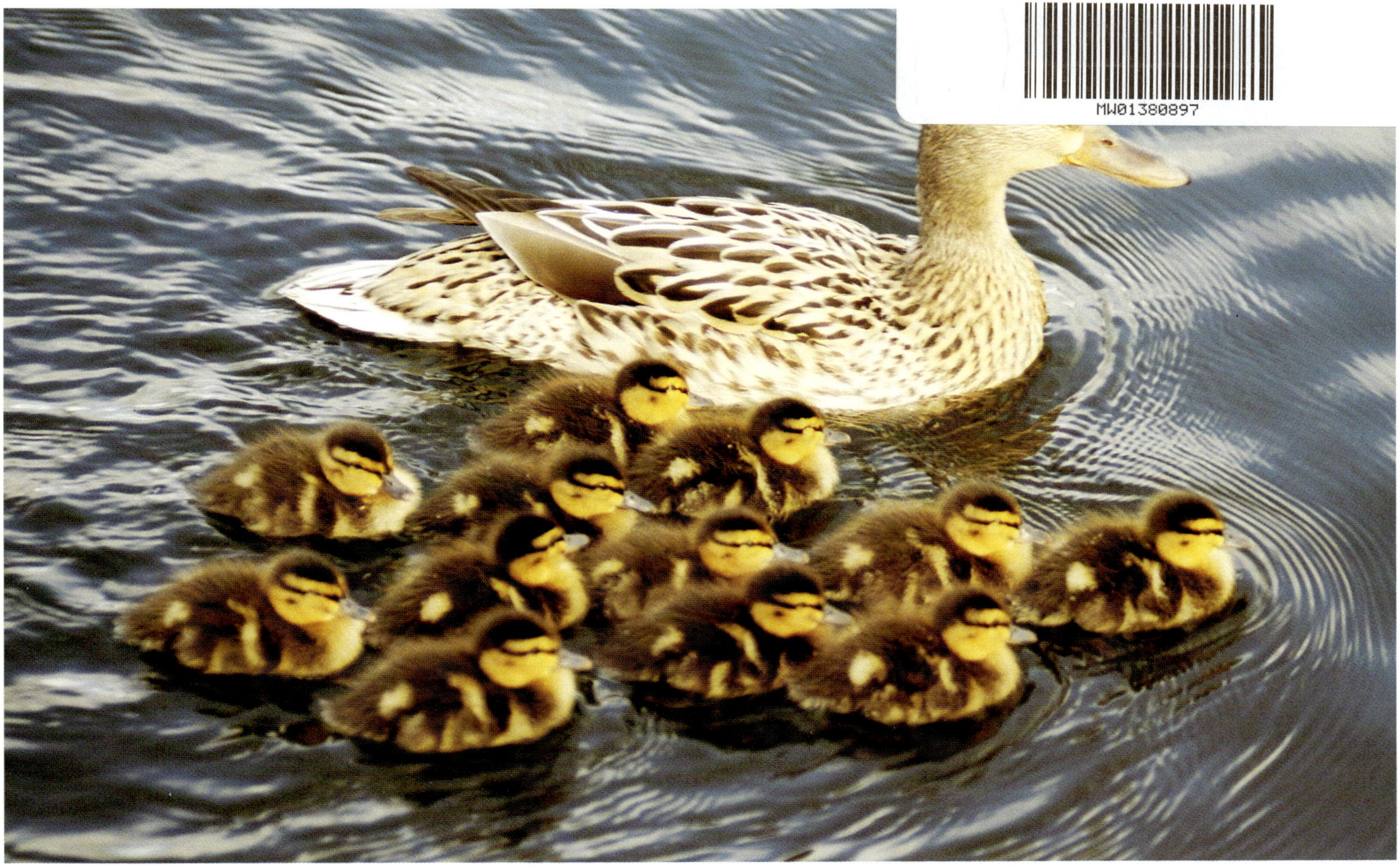

ducks

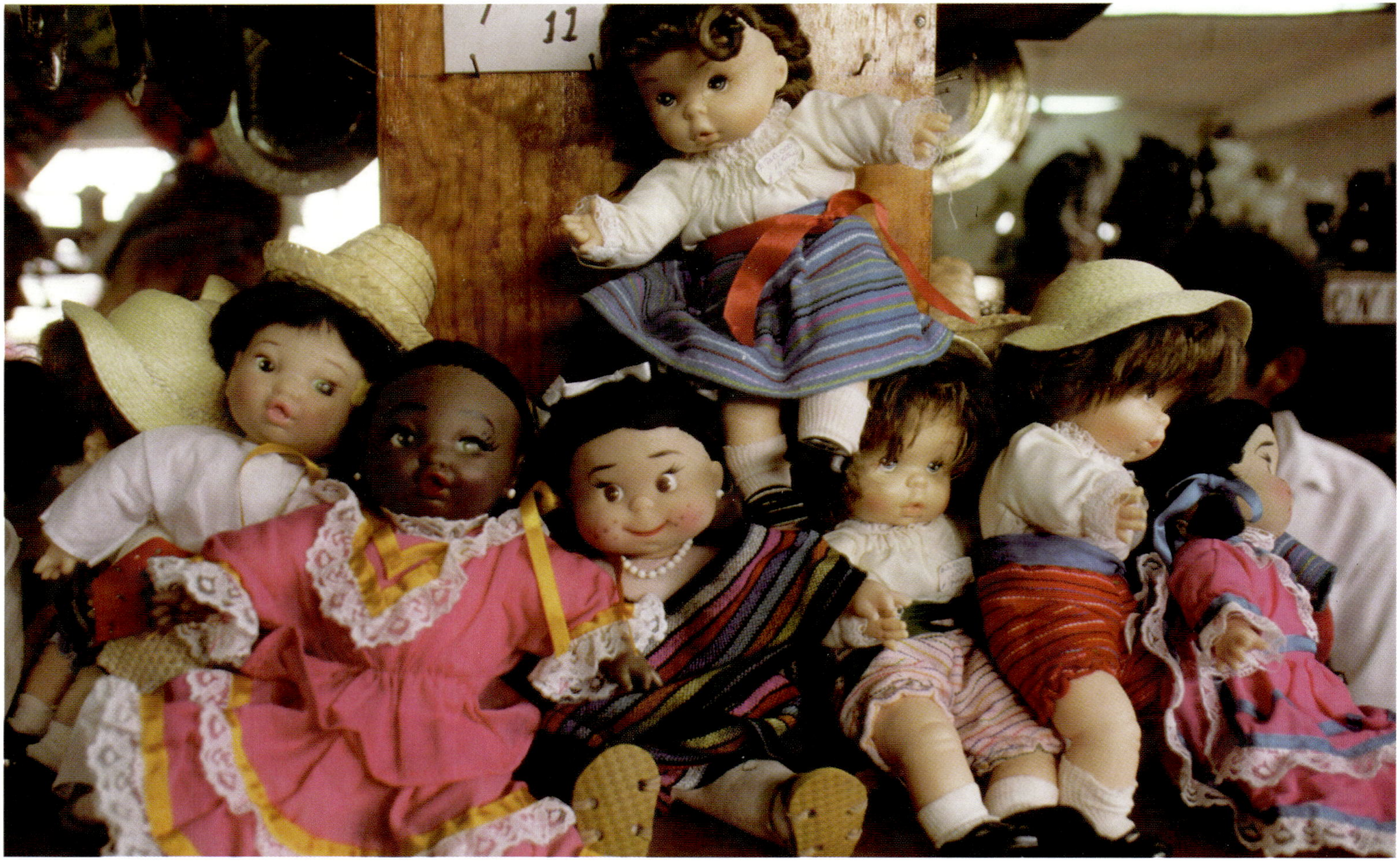

dolls

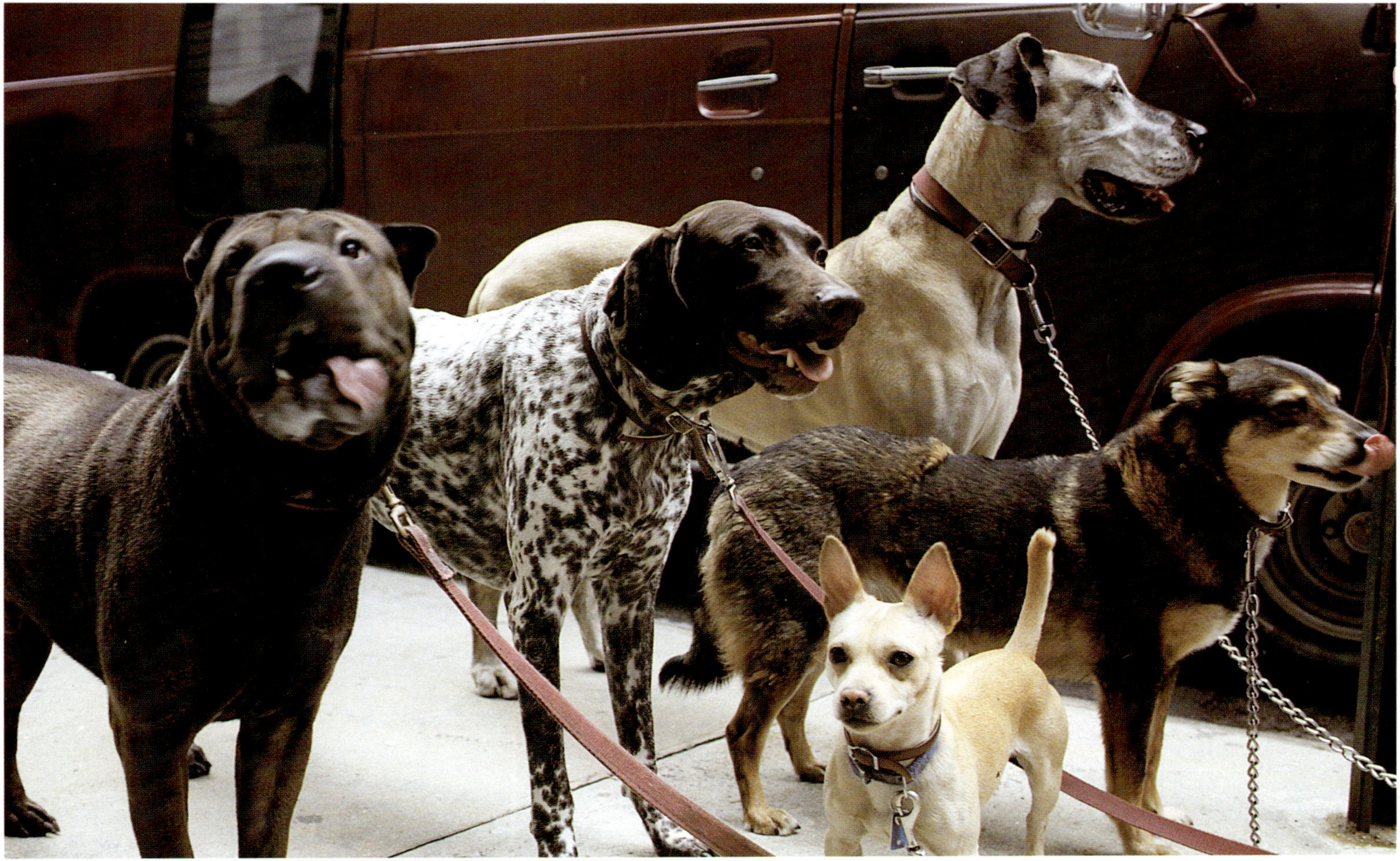

dogs

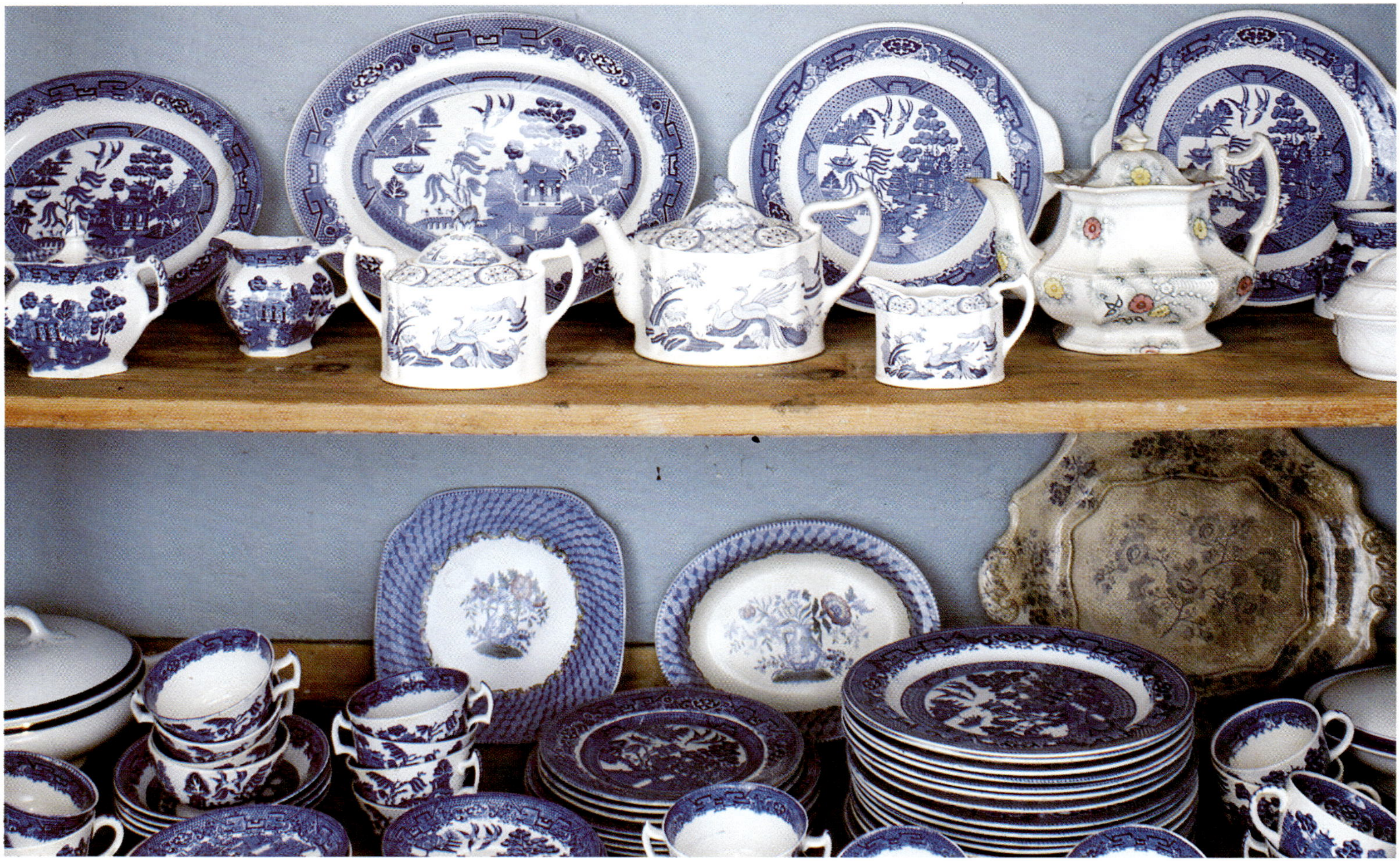

dishes

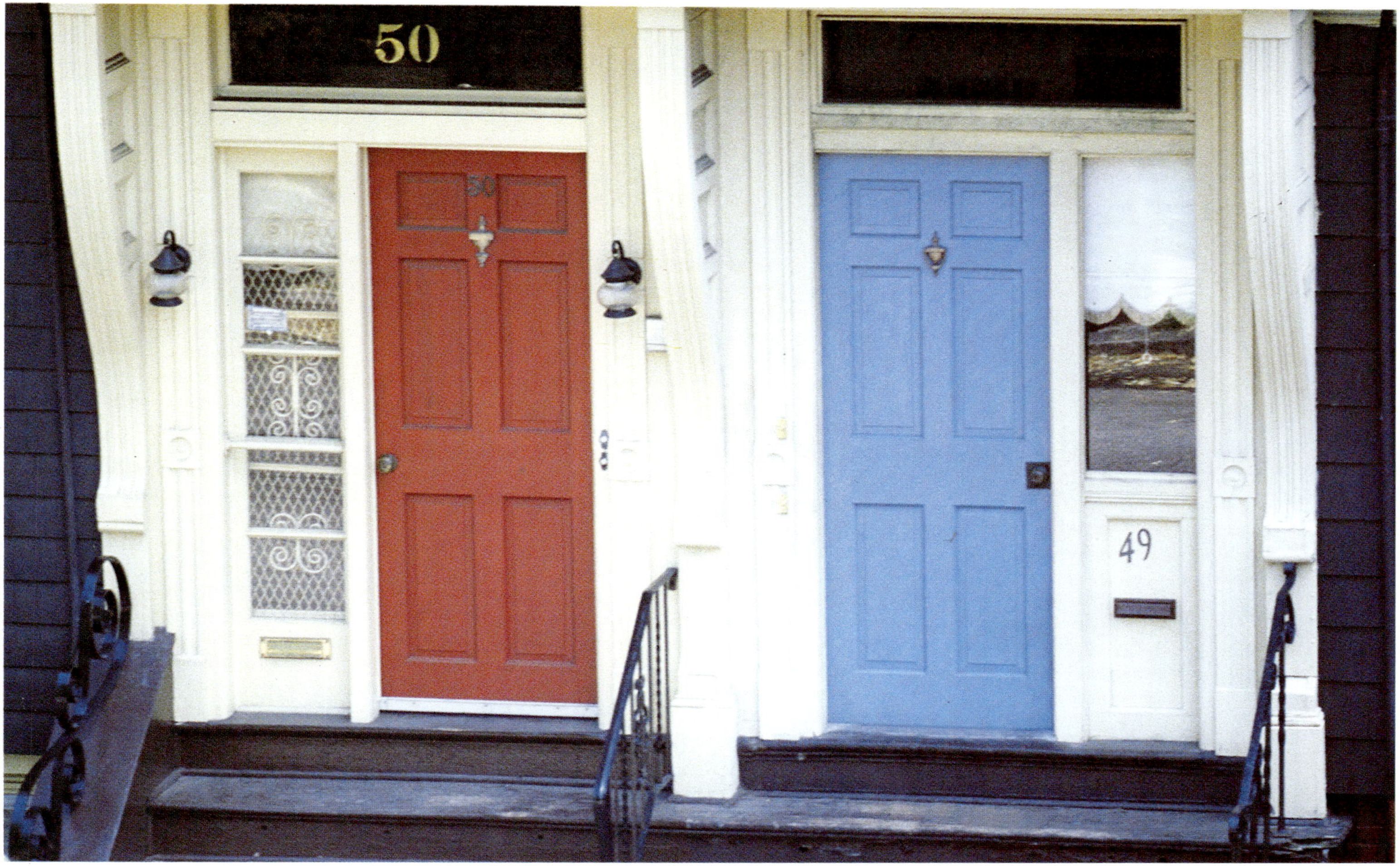

doors

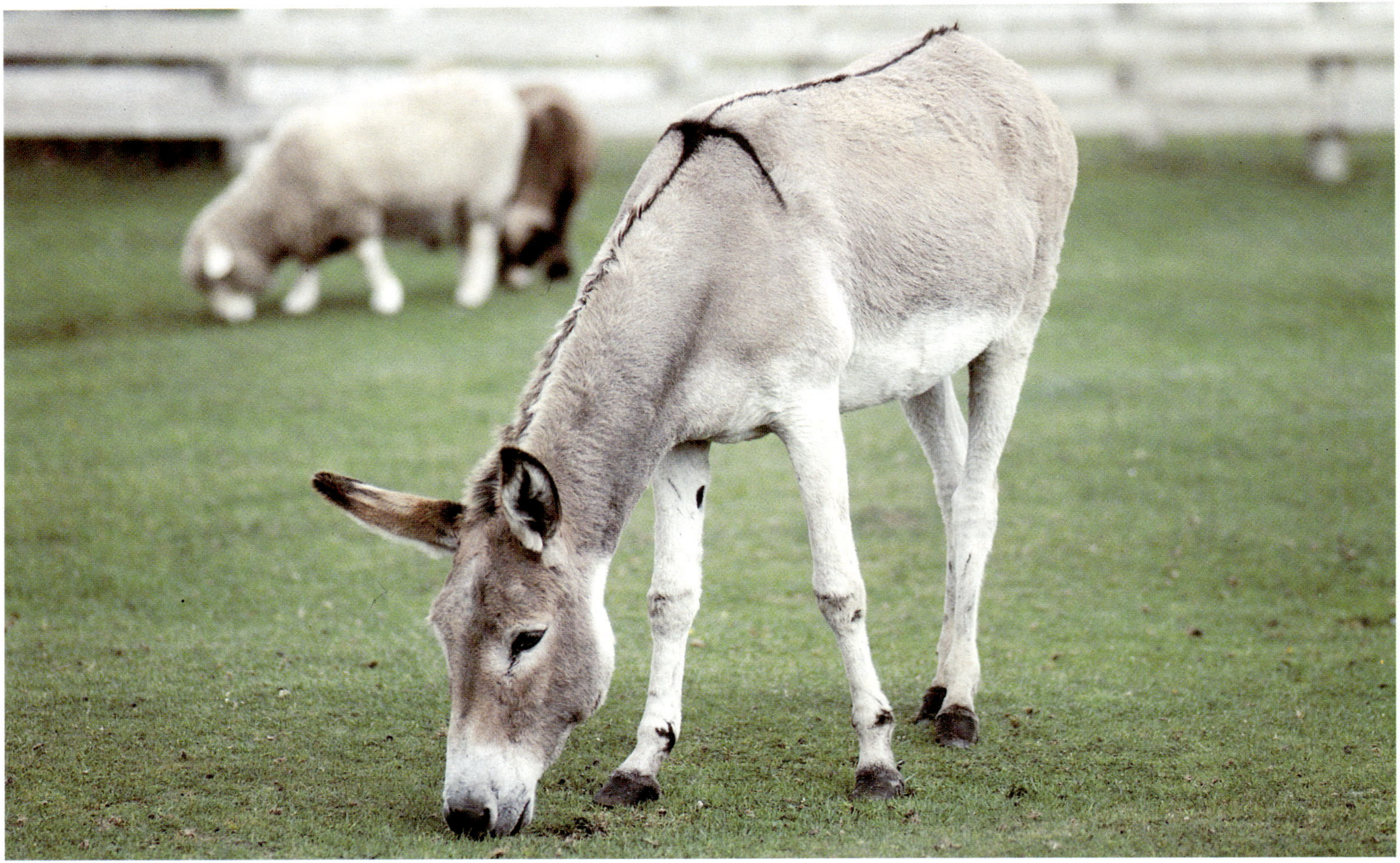

donkey

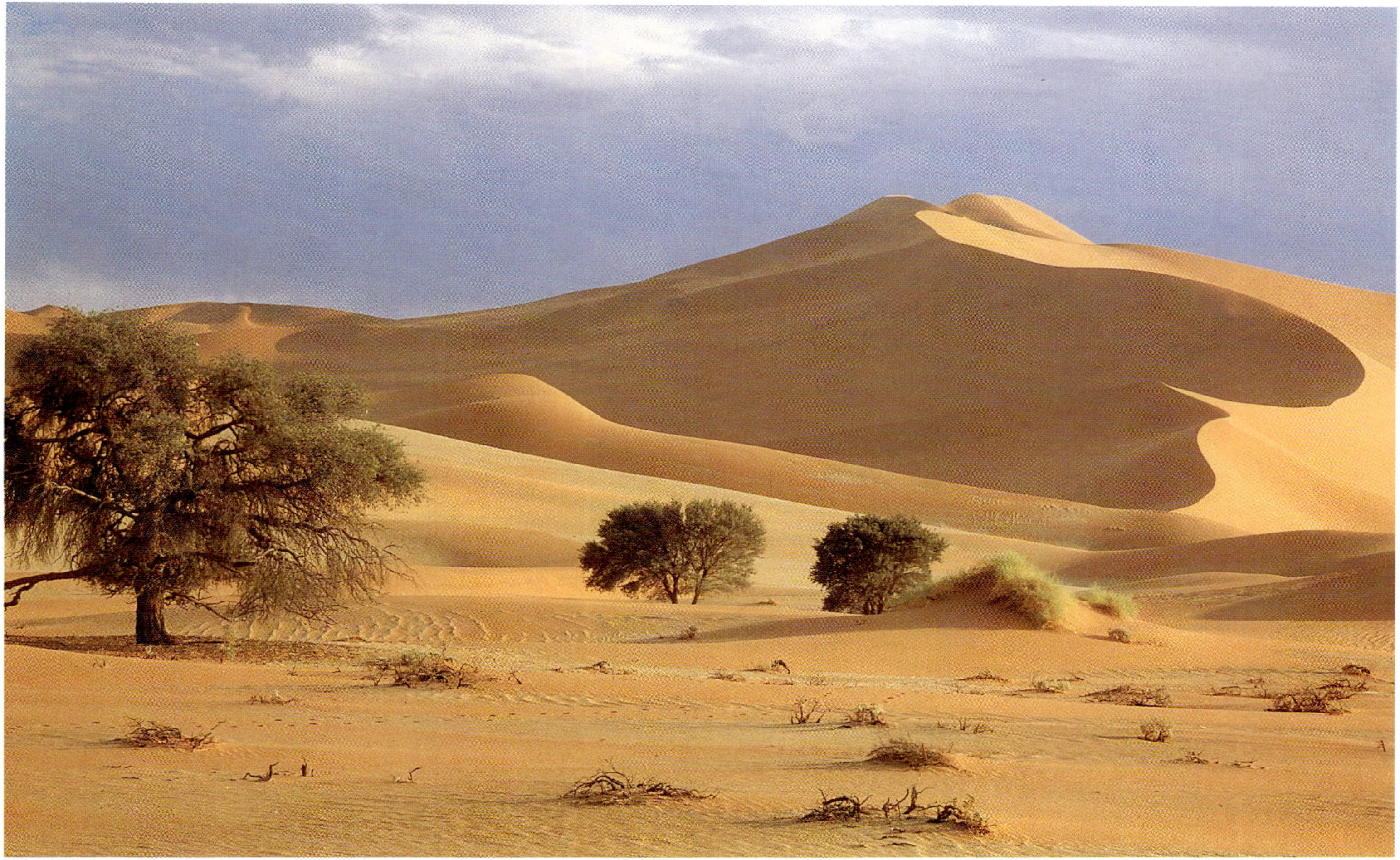

desert

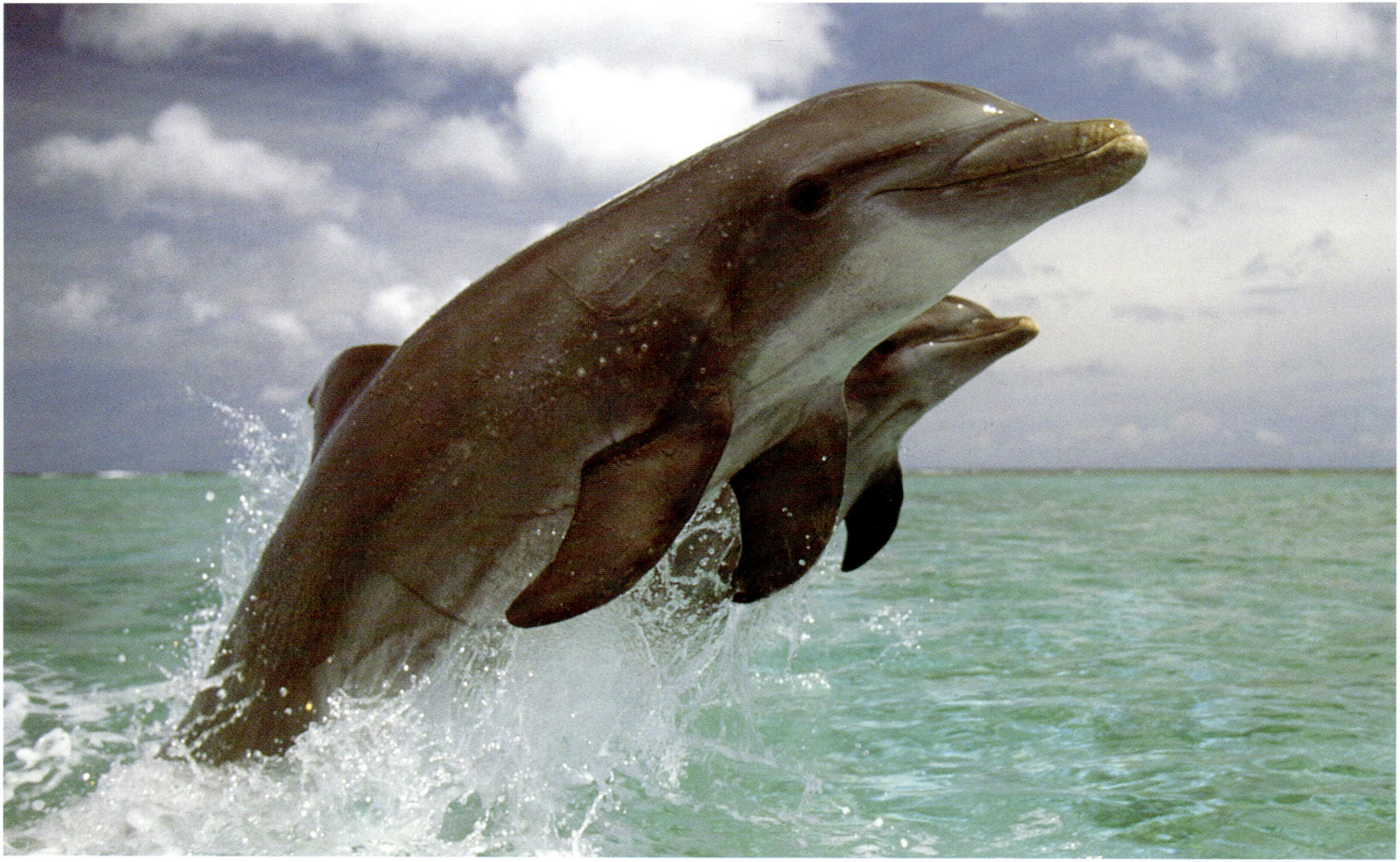

dolphins